FINALLY FREE
TO BE ME

Tamika Baldwin

© 2021 Divine Works Publishing
FINALLY FREE TO BE ME

All rights reserved. No part of this publication may be reproduced, stored in a retrieval system, or transmitted in any form or by any means, electronic, mechanical, photocopying, recording or otherwise without the prior permission of the publisher or in accordance with the provisions of the Copyright, Designs, and Patents Act 1988 or under the terms of any license permitting limited copying issued by the Copyright Licensing Agency.

The views expressed in this work are solely those of the author and do not necessarily reflect the views of the publisher, the publisher hereby disclaims any responsibility for them.

ISBN-13: 978-1-949105-35-3 (paperback)

Published by:
Divine Works Publishing
Royal Palm Beach, Florida USA
561-990-BOOK (2665)

www.DivineWorksPublishing.com

DEDICATION

This book is dedicated to my
Gifts from God

My Children:
Timothy, Jeremy, Shantera, and Gerald II

My Grandchildren:
Dreshawn, Christian, Londynn, Kailynn, Timothy Jr,
Tristian, and Chase Jeremiah

I Love You with all my Heart.

ACKNOWLEDGMENTS

Praise be to Abba Father for Gracing me with the opportunity to write *Finally Free to Be Me*. Thank you, Jesus, for calling me out of darkness into your marvelous light so that I may proclaim your praise in the earth realm. Thank you, Holy Spirit, for being my Comforter throughout the entire process of my healing and liberation.

Thank you to my mother and my bonus father Jane Mckeever and Vincent Mckeever for loving me and praying for my salvation.

To Hattie Bell Cooper, Grandma I love you more than words can ever express & to my grandfather, the late David Cooper—You are remembered today and always in my heart.

Special thanks to my siblings, Jamie and Craig Baldwin, for being my go-to people during the birthing of this book.

Thank you to my father, Raymond Baldwin, for your obedience in reconciling our relationship.

Last, but not least thank you to my four children and my uncle, Bobby Cooper, for believing in the dream to write this book. Dorothy Gregory for being my prayer partner. Sister Carrie Facan, for being my book sponsor, your gift is forever appreciated. Minister Darlene Davis Hord, founder of The Daughter's of Zion (DOZ) Mentorship Program and Minister Hildreth Brown, Mentor of DOZ, each one of you played a part in encouraging me to step out in faith to write *Finally Free to Be Me*.

CONTENTS

Preface *xi*

Chapter 1 | Defenseless Childhood Attack *1*

Chapter 2 | The Seed of the Enemy Grew *9*

Chapter 3 | Bittersweet Journey *19*

Chapter 4 | At the End of My Rope *31*

Chapter 5 | Rescued from the Hands of My Enemy *37*

Daily Prayer | Lord, Set Me Free to Be Me *49*

About the Author *51*

PREFACE
BACKDROP OF FINALLY FREE TO BE ME

The Oxford English Dictionary defines the word "Free" as; *not being under or in the power of another (meaning not or no longer confined or imprisoned)*. The opposite of Free is Captive; to be Captive means to be imprisoned; when someone is imprisoned they must be set Free... Thus, Luke 4: 18 Jesus came to set the Captives Free.

Finally Free to Be Me, is a written testimony about a young girl who grew up without her father—the man who should have been there to love and protect her—And how the void of his absence left her wide open to several traumatic encounters. The absence of her father also gave open access for the thief to come into her life. Who is the thief? His name is Satan. *The thief does not come except to steal, and to kill, and to destroy. I have come that they may have life, and that they may have it more abundantly* (John 10:10 NKJV).

The thief attacked her life at an early age and because of these childhood attacks, she now understands how Satan's agenda was meant to destroy her entire life. This young girl endured an extremely challenging childhood; those challenges and others continued throughout her adult life, so much so, that she became completely null and had no hope for any change—until one day the Father of all Fathers, God Almighty, came along and captured her with His Unconditional LOVE through His Son Jesus Christ. Jesus drew her in with His loving kindness and gave her exactly what she had always been missing, which was love and acceptance.

Once she was Captured by the Love of God, she was then given a New Life. *Therefore, if any man be in Christ, he is a new creature: old things are passed away: behold, all things are become new* (2 Corinthians 5:17 KJV), and because of this, the door that the thief entered through is now closed and he has no access to her life. Since her new life, she has been on a journey of healing from the mental and emotional effects of her past. She developed a passion to share her life's story for God to get the Glory. She believes that every person here on earth has a story; for we are all walking epistles. She also believes that there is power in telling our stories. As scripture declares, it provides freedom for everyone who hears and believes; *And they overcame Him by the blood of the Lamb, and by the word of their testimony* (Revelation 12:11 NKJV).

Her hopes and prayers are for teen girls, teen moms, young adult women, and hurting mothers to be set free. She has earnest wishes for all teenage girls, who are fatherless and who struggle in their identity and self-esteem, to find a safe place to express themselves and to understand they are not alone. She hopes to enlighten single parents of the mental and emotional struggles that result from a fatherless childhood. She prays that young adult women will come to know their worth early in life, and that hurting women would identify the root causes of why they are hurting (which may very well come from unresolved childhood trauma), but above all, she wants women to never give up or give in! No matter how much mess one may have in their lives; that same mess becomes an opportunity to become a messenger. Her core message is that freedom is readily available to those bound by the enemy's lies.

1

DEFENSELESS CHILDHOOD ATTACK

Imagine yourself as an innocent child under attack by the forces of darkness, i.e., Satan. You don't understand what's happening, nor are you able to express to anyone what's occurring. You are completely defenseless as this dark force pervades every part of your being; mind, body, soul, and spirit. I don't know about you, but when I think about how pure and innocent children are, it saddens my heart to think about such things and my immediate thoughts are that I would want that person held accountable for his/her evil actions. I would confront them and/or expose them to the proper authorities. Now granted, these are the steps I would think to take if I were speaking of or dealing with a natural human being. However, in this case I am speaking of Satan—who is a spirit being, that is not seen with the natural eyes and can only be exposed by the Spirit of Truth and Light (Jesus Christ). Satan is a defeated foe; yet he attempts to target and attack the defenseless ones; he's a thief, a liar, a murder, and a destroyer. He is a coward that does not fight fair. He peaks into the future of God's creation; he sees the divine plan of God for them, then he plots against their very purpose and destiny. How do I know this? Well, because I have evidence and a series of personal experiences which lead me to believe that one of his main goals is to sabotage the pureness of one's mind and emotions from the moment one is conceived in the womb, and by the time we exit the womb he's fully ready to release his destructive plans to kill, steal, and destroy—*The thief comes only to steal, kill, and destroy; I have come that they may have life, and have it to the full. –John 10:10 NIV*—their destiny. Why? Simply because he knows they are God's masterpieces.

For we are God's masterpiece –Ephesians 2:10 NIV.

He has created us anew in Christ Jesus so we can do the good things He planned for us long ago. Satan's plans are to block one's abilities to become who GOD predestined them to be. Please note that I said block and not stop. You will understand this statement later in another chapter. In the meantime, allow me to begin the journey of unfolding my story to you.

The above opening summary of this chapter *Defenseless Childhood Attack* was intended to engage your imagination and prepare you to travel along with me throughout the rest of this book, as I detail the course of my personal journey and vulnerably share how God used the good, and not so good, in my life for his purposes (Romans 8:28). The idea for this derived via a Women's Prayer Breakfast I attended along with my church family, a year or so after receiving my salvation in 2010. That gathering impacted my life so much that I remember that day like it was yesterday. I remembered the speaker was a very special female evangelist. The scripture she taught on was Jeremiah 29:11. At the end of that service, she conducted an altar call for prayer. Because I was young in the Lord, I waited for my First Lady to approach the altar before I went (you know, kind of like a child's response with their parent; if the child sees a parent approaching an area as a safe place they're willing to trust that it's safe to do so as well) once my First Lady went, I followed. The woman of God began praying for everyone who came to the altar. When she reached me, she stopped and looked for a moment and then prayed. While she was praying, she said to me "from the moment you exited your mother's womb the devil tried to kill you" and then she walked away. I recall thinking "what is she talking about?" Well I can now testify that it's true. God truly discerns the thoughts of men/women. God directed her to come right back and say, "young lady even during your teenage years Satan robbed you," NOW that connected with me and deeply touched my heart because it was the truth about my teenage years. She said, "sweetheart you got a purpose over your life, although you don't know it right now nor do you understand it; you got it;" she continued on "sweetheart you walk with purpose." Outwardly, I lifted my hands and began thanking God; but inwardly I was fighting back tears. God led her to deal with something deep down on the inside of me. It was true, my life as a teenager was abnormal, so I knew it was God speaking through her. I was happy for the prophecy and encouragement, but upon returning home her words replayed in my mind "from the moment you exited your Mother's womb the devil tried to kill you."

    I rushed home, headed straight to the bathroom, got on my knees, and prayed that night. I asked God why my life was the way it was. The tears I held back at the altar now flooded my bathroom floor. I couldn't help but release them as I questioned God about the part of my life which seemed to be void (around the age of 11 and under) and the part that I did recall which was from 12 and up. I cried and prayed until eventually I fell asleep.

The next morning, I awoke bright and early while an array of unanswered thoughts and questions bombarded my mind. I was curious about why the devil attacked me at such an early age and then throughout my entire life. So, I called my grandmother (who helped raise me), and I asked her to explain what happened in my life before age 12. She was the type of person who would shield me from the impact of things, so she attempted to change the subject by replying "You are saved now, just keep looking to God, because some things are best left alone." I sat quietly as I struggled to find the words to inform her I wasn't asking because I wanted to know, but because I needed to know. Before I could respond, she shifted from avoiding the conversation and began sharing things I had heard her say before, but honestly never paid attention to. However, on this particular day, as she spoke about an incident which occurred while I was between the ages of 5-7, the latter part of what she said hit me hard. She explained that I had been hospitalized, and one day during my stay at the hospital, she stopped by to visit me and as she walked in the room, there was a man who professed to be a Prophet of God praying over me. He had apparently said, God was saying, I was going to die and that my mother should prepare for it. My grandmother informed me that she boldly commanded him to leave. At this, he rebuked her, saying she disrespected his God-given authority, but she stood her ground and requested he immediately leave.

My grandmother also explained how frightened I became whenever any type of violent behavior erupted in our home, or amongst our family members, and how I would hide myself during those times. She also informed me that I suffered intense migraine headaches as a child. She then shifted once again and resumed her normal way of joking and ended our call.

Immediately after that phone call, the memory of my father being absent in my life became fully alive. Overwhelming feelings of rejection and abandonment which had become painfully suppressed memories suddenly surfaced. I recalled my father promising me a pink and white birthday cake for my 9th birthday that I never received. It was at that moment I realized how deeply this incident affected me and taught me to not trust in promises. It also became the subconscious reason I disliked the color pink.

I also had a visual in my mind of being at an office with my mother and grandmother, and during that office visit, my mother looked deeply hurt and disappointed. Although she never once uttered a word about it, I could see the hurt in her eyes. I later received the revelation of what that office was; it was the child support office, and that explained why I always felt in my heart that child support was an unhealthy choice.

God provided answers to my many questions; those answers helped me to gain clarity as I became fully aware that Satan was real and that he gained access to my life from a very young age. Becoming aware of this reminded me of a sermon I once heard entitled Stay Daddy Stay: Don't let Satan have his way. That message was about how the absence of a father gives the thief access to enter a child's life. Answers to my questions were being spoken loud and clear as God gave me an understanding of the how and why the thief entered my life. The absence of my father gave him access to the door of my mind, which could not comprehend a father leaving his baby girl. The door of my heart that longed to experience the love of her father and to hear him whisper words like I was his little princess. The thief {Satan} targeted my mind and emotions. His aim was to successfully destroy my purpose here on Earth with his attacks by delivering corrupt seeds in my soul, which grew and developed, causing me to embrace dysfunctional behaviors which ultimately produced toxic cycles in my life. As I discovered the knowledge of how and why Satan attacked my life, all I could do was lay in a fetal position weeping and crying out, "God, why me?"

Although I had the knowledge of what happened and the reasons it happened, I still had not yet come to a complete understanding that from the beginning of time, God was fully aware of everything that happened in my life. Nor did I know how much He loved me and His grand plans for me, like this right now—writing my story of freedom for His Glory. Upon the writing of this book, I believe that the way my life story is unfolding was not God's original plan, however, because He always has a backup plan, He was ready and willing to take my mess and turn it into His message. That's why He said what the enemy meant for evil; God meant it for my good (Genesis 50:20 KJV). This scripture reminds me of lyrics to a song called *He turned it*, by Tye Tribuett. It says, "The devil thought he had me; He thought my life was over; He thought by now I'd give up; He thought I had no more, But that's when someone greater stepped in my situation. My morning has now begun; He turned it!" The enemy attacked me at birth, he planted corruptible seeds, those seeds grew. For years I struggled with the seeds planted in me. I call them issues but Jesus, in his timing, stepped in and turned it; Hallelujah HE TURNED IT...

Listen, I feel myself moving to a praise that will most likely cause me to move ahead of God and not follow the direct order of this book. So I am going to end this chapter by saying when Satan attacks, He doesn't care about age, color, gender, or race. He has no limit to what he will do to get his job done, which is to steal, kill, and destroy your life. He targets anyone; man, woman, boy, or girl. I was a precious, innocent little girl when he peeked into my future and saw

God's destiny for me and then he plotted his wicked plans to plant toxic seeds, which led me into being a troubled child with delinquent behaviors. The separation of my parents delivered a seed of rejection and abandonment, the violent behavior I witnessed delivered seeds of fear, hate, and anger. The spoken words of death delivered mental torment. All of this combined launched me towards a path of destruction and believe me, it took many years for me to turn from that path. You will witness the years it took as you continue to explore the journey of my story for God's Glory. I beseech you to praise the Lord with me as I share the next chapter in preparing you to understand why I can say with assurance I Am Finally Free To Be Me!

2

THE SEED OF THE ENEMY GREW

Once seeds are planted, they grow, and when they grow they reproduce. A reproduction of seeds from the enemy grew in my life from early childhood (rejection, abandonment, and fear). Those seeds caused me mental and emotional instability. This led to destructive behaviors and down a destructive path. By the age of 12, more seeds were implanted, for example, the seed of lust as I stumbled across porn magazines that were in the bathroom cabinets at a family member's house, an older man attempting to molest me while I slept (but his plan wasn't successful), and an older male whom I knew very well and trusted somehow ended up in a bed with me performing actions that were meant in a sexual way. Although I don't recall everything about that moment, I'm left with no choice but to believe that this occurred more than once—simply because the memories that I do have about the incident reflect that I felt comfortable and at ease during the inappropriate behavior. The wrongful behavior of these men watered the seed of promiscuity (the act of engaging in immoral sexual activities). Some studies say that promiscuity results from not having a father present while growing up.

The seeds of lying and stealing were also deposited into my life as I grew up around family members who were broken and lived addictive lifestyles inclusive of stealing, lying, and drugs, that led them repeatedly in and out of jail. Back in the 70s, 80s, and early 90s families would not readily admit that those behaviors were abnormal and defined as dysfunctional behaviors. According to Merriam–Webster dysfunctional is defined as: Impaired or abnormal. Having grown up in a dysfunctional environment led me into a toxic cycle of learned behaviors and generational bondage. Let me clear the air here. This is not intended to paint a bad picture of my family. This is all about telling the truth about becoming Finally Free to be me; nothing less and nothing more. I have an inward (heart) posture to Give God all the Glory for no man can share His Glory (I am the Lord; that is my name! I will not yield my glory to another or my praise to idols. -Isaiah 42:8 NIV) Okay, now that I have cleared the air shall I continue? Having dealt with the first form of rejection and abandonment from the absence of my father caused rejection to show up in many forms.

During the summer of age 12, I joined a cheerleading team in the local community where I lived and towards the end of that season I was presented with an opportunity to run for homecoming queen, the decision of the winners was supposed to be determined by who raised the most money; I came in third place not because of finances, but because of favoritism (another form of rejection).

I overheard some adults speaking about the fact that I raised more money than the second runner-up, but I grew up in the days and times when children were taught to shut their mouths and respect elders so that's exactly what I did. However, upon hearing that conversation wounded me and left me open to forming beliefs that I was not worthy enough to be first or second choice but that instead I was worthy of being last. It taught me to suppress my feelings when someone did things that I did not like, or even that I knew were wrong. The result of that hurt led to me growing up with a dislike for those who showed favoritism and later on it hindered me in many other areas of my life.

By age 12, I unknowingly suffered from depression, deep-seated insecurities, and chronic low self-esteem. I also lacked emotional stability. I battled emotionally on many days feeling different from others. It seemed as if I continuously encountered people who rejected me or who judged me according to my skin complexion and those who misinterpreted my innate nature of not being a fighter as a pushover. For example, one day a young girl stabbed me in my face with a pencil. Until this day, I don't know why she had issues with me. Despite her cruel actions, I never held this incident against her, nor did I treat her any differently. This is just one of many examples why I felt rejected, different, or didn't fit in. Now granted, chances are maybe I did and just didn't know how to.

At some point, I discovered a flicker joy in helping others, so I spent a lot of time babysitting the kids who lived next door to me. All three of them were a few years younger than me and it felt good to help them. I felt like their parents, who worked, needed me; those parents entrusted me with their kids so I always did my very best for them. I also met two new friends who lived around the corner from me. They were always kind to me. Their family attended church and sometimes I would go with them. I even sang with them at a few Christmas gatherings, but even being with them I felt out of place. However, as much as I enjoyed babysitting those kids and hanging around my two church friends, all of that quickly became boring to me and soon after I developed an interest in hanging around older girls (between the ages of 14 through 16). Upon returning to school, I found that group of girls, I befriended them and in doing so my attitude, behavior, and desires took a 180 degree turn and it wasn't for the better; as strange as it may sound, it felt like I "connected" with them. Once again, please hear my heart as I clear the air, this story is not written to project a bad image of others. Looking back now I can clearly see why I felt that way, it was because we all had the same seeds of rejection and abandonment from our fathers working within us.

Not long after l began hanging out with that older group of girls was I exposed to skipping classes which eventually led to leaving the school campus. One day led to everyday. Each day we had two certain stops when we left school #1 was the ice skating arena to steal money out of the skaters lockers (remember, I stated I grew up around people who would steal, this seed manifested during that time), and #2 any local retail store to steal clothing and shoes. My main reasons were so that I would not feel embarrassed around the other young girls who wore the latest fashions. During that phase of my life, there was an occasion whereby I was arrested and because I was a juvenile, my parents had to pick me up. By this time, I had frustrated my mother with my ongoing behaviors and she elected to not come for me. I felt rejected and confused when my mother said she was not coming to get me. In my mind I was thinking, I was her only girl, and I felt she should have picked me up. As a child, I'm telling you although my actions were wrong, the already contaminated seeds in my mind and heart perceived that as rejection from my mother. I believe that situation only made matters worse. Thereafter I did not leave school campus for a while but on the days I went to school I would act out in class so much that the principal knew my name like a psalmist knows their song.

She always quoted these words to me, "Ms. Baldwin, get to class or Ms. Baldwin, I am putting you in detention and from there you are going home for 3 days". Like any other troubled kid, I would plead for forgiveness, receive it, and then go right back to doing the same things; only the same things seemed to increase to worse issues, for example the desire of wanting to date boys.

That desire was for filled by flirting around with boys and entertaining the pre-cursors of sex like kissing, touching, and feeling. Shortly after that I ran away from home countless times, which resulted in taking a trip to a group home facility where I had to stay for thirty days along with other young teens; some of whom were already young mothers. However, I even ran away from that place and because of this they assigned me a school counselor. He was an older man who always wore boots and a hat. He and my school's principal both had one thing in common, and that was calling me Ms. Baldwin. Only his words were "Ms. Baldwin, what am I going to do with you, you just don't seem to get it". These words were spoken because my behavior kept getting worse; my attendance was next to zero and to make matters worse, I had gotten into a fight with an 8th grader. That fight went totally left field. She and I had a few licks, and it was over; at least to her and I it was, but for the crowd I hung out with it wasn't, so that fight got out of control to the point of that young girl having to be taken to the ER. Because of this, the next morning the school's principal and my counselor called me out of my first period class into the office. I was asked to have a seat and wait until my mother arrived, not knowing that the reason my mom was called into the school was because the young girl's grandmother was waiting in another office and came to report that she had to take her granddaughter to the ER. The fight left her with a fractured arm.

Although this happened after school, and it took place a few feet away from the school campus, her grandmother commanded consequences for my actions. So, this brought up the discussion of me being expelled from school. Well, as much as I thought the principal and my counselor didn't like me because of my behavior, they always seemed to go the extra mile to help me. My counselor suggested that my mother remove me from that school and send me to another school just a few miles away; my mother agreed and off to the other school I went. That transition was tough for me because I had become used to being with my friends and doing what we did best—which was skipping school to have what "we" considered fun. And to add to that, I was yet again around peers that I felt totally different from, and that catching up with my grades was very challenging. However, I made an effort to do so. I was attending class and slowly getting my academic levels up until I became a target of another student's abusive behavior (nowadays it's called bullying) this young girl had it out for me. She would follow me in the hallway, push me in the back, and try to trip me in hopes of me falling flat on my face. I was so fearful of her I stopped going to school. My attendance was so bad that the school called home and commanded my mother to come to the school for a meeting. Being that my mother could not take off from work, my grandmother attended that meeting. I could then justify my choice to not attend school. My Grandmother discovered I wasn't that student's first victim, she had a history of targeting other kids before. My grandmother made sure that I was her last victim, so she took me to the court house and filed for a restraining order and within a month we received a court date and the judge ruled in my favor. He ordered that young girl to stay away from me {later on in life I found out that she was also a victim of rejection because of her mother being deceased and her father was not present and that was her way of acting out}. By now it's the end of 7th grade. School was about to be closed for the summer, so I went back to hanging out with my former friends. During this time, I met a young guy who lived near my neighborhood. We began hanging out regularly. Our meetings led to us becoming sexually active. Our choice to do so came with a consequence. Do you recall my prior statement about taking a trip to a group home and at that group home there were some young moms? Well, I believe that was a warning for me which I did not heed to. Here's why... About two months after becoming sexually active with this guy, guess who was pregnant? "Yes' ' it was me, 13 and Pregnant.

One day after I went to the restroom at my aunt's house because of having stomach pains and bleeding. It frightened me so much that I screamed out loud. My aunt rushed into the restroom to see what was going on, and then she called my mother at work. My mother came to my aunt's house right away and took me to the nearest hospital in the Fort Lauderdale area where my aunt lived. Then came the news no parent wants to hear about their 13-year-old daughter "Mrs. Baldwin, your daughter is pregnant, and she is having a miscarriage". The Doctor then explained to my mother that he would need to do a DNC (A DNC is a procedure that's preformed to remove tissue from inside of your uterus or to clear the uterine lining after a miscarriage or abortion) in my case I was having a miscarriage. The nurse on duty entered the room to bring papers for my mother to sign. I could see the concerned look in my mother's eye when she had to read and sign the papers that had information on the procedure the doctor would perform, all the side effects, and everything that could become a risk or at the worst long-term damage. Her eyes held back the three P's, and those were PAIN, PAIN, AND MORE PAIN.. Immediately after she signed, The DNC procedure was completed and in within a few hours off to home my mother and I went along with instructions to rest for a few days and follow up with my primary doctor within two weeks. However, before the two weeks were up, I had become sick. I vomited blood, so my mother took me back to the same hospital. The doctor ordered several tests, including one that required me to have a tube inserted through my nose that went down to my stomach to discover what was causing the bleeding. I recall being so scared that three nurses and my mother had to attend the process of that test. All of my tests came back and of course the pregnancy test was now negative because of the miscarriage, my blood count was overall good, my iron was low but not enough to be concerned about but a few minutes later the nurse came into the room and says MOM the doctor is going to have to admit your daughter apparently there's a concern that a portion of the fetus may still be there and he may have to perform another DNC, but before he does, he would like to watch her for at least 48 hours. After being admitted later that night, whatever was there came out while I used the restroom. Until this point, my mother had not questioned who I was pregnant from. I believe it was because of the mental process of it all. During my hospital stay she looked at me with a look that as if she appeared to be exhausted from all my troubled behaviors. She then asked me "where's the guy who with child you?" She said she needed to see him and his parents. I told her who he was, she called him and his mother. I don't know what was said, but I know they showed up at the hospital and the entire time they were both supportive. Amid this timing, he and his mother found out that I had lied (there's that seed that I said I was raised around) to him about my age. He thought I was 16 going 17. After finding out my age, his mother boldly said to us we didn't need to see each other again. My mother agreed and made it clear to us we should not see each other any more. So that was the end of our so-called relationship. I recovered from that DNC procedure. After all that I had been through you would think that by now I had learned and was fully ready to follow a different path, but there was still no improvement. You would think that the seeds in me would have died by now; well truth is that's not the case; the enemy had executed his plans during my early childhood years and his plans had succeeded. The corrupted seeds he planted were growing and reproducing a rapid harvest straight towards the path of destruction, and I followed that path.

    I went back to doing the same things. Everything became more intense in my life. As a result, I got worse with skipping school and running away from home. I was totally disobedient and rebellious towards all parental advice in my life and to anyone in authority. My life was fully under the control of bad choices, which led me to deal with consequences I was ill-prepared to handle. You may think, how much worse are you talking about? I challenge you to take a few seconds and think about what the next chapter will reveal. Some of you may be right on target, some of you may hit the mark closely, some of you may be totally off. I hope that whatever you have guessed engages your excitement. To discover if your thoughts are correct. Selah!

    Shall we continue....

3

BITTERSWEET JOURNEY

Collins dictionary states that the word bittersweet is described as an experience that means that it has some happy aspects and some not so happy ones. My bittersweet journey started on October 26, 1990. That day changed the course of my life for over 20-plus years. I will never forget that day. It was a Friday evening around 7 pm; I was hanging outside at the apartment complex where I lived. One of the girls who lived upstairs from me held a gathering in celebration of her 14th birthday. That gathering drew many young people together. We all stood outside and socialized with one another. I was always the one to stand off from the crowd, so that night as I stood behind the back end of a car in the parking lot, I gazed into the eyes of a dark-skinned, well-dressed guy. After our eyes connected, it seemed as if our souls were immediately drawn together. Please don't laugh at what I'm about to say next, but the truth is that I hit on him first by telling him how handsome he was. That opened the door for a conversation between him and I. He smiled with great confidence, being assured of himself as some would say, and a few minutes later we both went upstairs to join the party. We danced and shortly after, we went back outside. He gave me his beeper number to reach him, but in the back of my mind I was thinking I'm not going to contact him. Well that thought exited my head by the dawning of the new day. I woke up with him on my mind, so I ended up contacting him. We met up to talk. A part of our conversation was the sharing of our ages. He was 19, and I was 16 at least that's what I had told him unfortunately the truth is that I wasn't honest about my age. I told him that I was 16 going on 17, but I was only 14. Throughout our conversation we never talked about dating, but from that day on we started seeing each other every day. I would wake up and get dressed for school but never once made it to school because I met up with him instead to hang out. Our relationship progressed quickly and by mid-November he asked me to have his baby. I didn't think twice; I quickly responded by saying "Yes". The choice to have a baby was set in stone. We both agreed and tried every given chance to make that happen. We'd then go to the clinic to get tested.

  This shows both the innocence and ignorance of what we had chosen to do because clearly no one tries to have a baby and goes get tested the next two or three days and expects to receive positive results. Our common sense should have let us know that it takes a few weeks to get the most accurate answer, but it didn't, so we keep up the cycle of trying and then being tested a couple days thereafter; only to get the same negative result. This continued until one day we were talking with a close friend of his who suggested we try a pill that would help us plan to have a baby. For the protection of the minds and hearts of any teen or young adult that may be reading this book, I will not disclose the name of that pill. All that needs to be known is that I took that pill and the next clinic visit was in January 1991 and at that visit I discovered I was pregnant. Fourteen and pregnant again. I said again because as you read in chapter two I revealed I was pregnant at age 13, but I had a miscarriage. Well, this time there was no miscarriage. Now let's recap. I met this guy in October 1990 and was pregnant by January 1991. If you do the math correctly, this reveals that I was pregnant within two months. It also clarifies what I meant when I stated that our relationship moved really fast...

Now, please know that I am fully aware of the many responses to this truth. I envision that some people reading this book may at this moment have their eyebrows turned in together, you know that facial frown people make when thinking thoughts that sound something like this "she must have sleep with him during the first week of meeting him or I should have been her mama for just one day and when I had finished with her, she would not have even thought about sleeping around again, or she should have been ashamed of herself and/or had her some more respect for herself than that". While all those thoughts may be true; what is also true is that I was not the first nor will I be the last, but I am one who has gracefully survived and evolved to share my story in hopes of helping others avoid some of these same pitfalls. Being pregnant at fourteen was extremely challenging. I dealt with morning sickness and severe hormonal fluctuations during the early stages of my pregnancy. I dealt with shame and embarrassment, separation and isolation, as I came in contact with the negative talk of older adults who assumed that I couldn't hear nor understand their form of negative communications. Things like "she's too fast for me", or "my child can't hang around her", or even the simple five word statement "WOW, just look at her!" I also struggled to continue with school so I eventually lost all interest and dropped out in the first semester of 9th grade. Just three months after my fifteenth birthday, I gave birth to my first born (A

Baby Boy). He was born on September 15, 1991. I do not remember everything about the birthing process, but I do remember that an older lady told me that life is not about you anymore, and boy did I not know what she meant until years later. However, that statement never left my thoughts. Shortly after I gave birth to my son, I moved out of my mother's house because I did not want to follow her rules. It was fun in the beginning, but then life got real as I had to endure sleepless nights with my child and several doctor's appointments because my son suffered from a common stomach problem called acid reflux. This was so bad at times that he had to be hospitalized on many visits to the doctors. Living with others was also incredibly stressful, but I used cleaning to deal with that stress; for some reason, I always found cleaning comforting. I experienced several hardships and several successes as I managed being a teenager, a mom, and a lover—and at some point, a working mom. I was young and immature, so I handled a lot of situations in childish ways, especially pertaining to my partner as we faced the numerous trials young people do. The things we experienced were more than enough reasons for me to make the choice to not have another baby and or to do better for myself, so that my life could possibly be different. I was an emotional person under stress and I had not yet learned how to be a successful mother to my first born, and in spite of those facts, two years later I became pregnant. Seventeen years old, a high school dropout, and pregnant again. Can I be permitted to say that even at age 17 I still didn't mentally get what was going on; I promise you this is true; it's like I wasn't able to comprehend everything that was taking place in my life, however the forward side of this statement is that I am aware that Satan simply was not playing fair in my life. He showed absolutely no pity. My second pregnancy was totally different from my first due to the emotional distress that I was experiencing. The doctors suggested that I consider taking some important measures such as different tests and so forth; however, somehow I had this thought that told me to not follow through with those tests and that my baby was going to be just fine. Sure enough, I gave birth to a healthy baby boy, born on February 22, 1994. I was so happy that I listened to that thought.

Being a mother times two and maintaining my relationship with their father was extremely challenging at times. I had a lot of trust issues due to several encounters that brought my heart to the point of not trusting anyone, including him. Therefore, we did a lot of breaking up and coming back together. I tried to balance my life at all times. My heart always wanted to make sure that my kid's life differed from mine as a child—meaning fatherless and heartbroken; I did not know that it wasn't as easy as I thought. I did not know that I needed to be healed from the wounds of rejection and abandonment. I didn't know my wounds caused me to act out physically. For example, I fought with my mouth. Whatever came up came out; in other words, I could be verbally abusive, which is also considered a form of rage. My partner and I broke up many times because of it, but no matter how many times we broke up, we just kept getting back together, especially sexually. After my second pregnancy, I became pregnant again. During that time, he and I were going through one of our "changes" as I like to call it. Someone dear to us had just had an abortion, and she knew what we were going through, so she gave me the information needed to have an abortion. The next day I made an appointment. I was so scared to do it, because I knew in my heart that it was not right plus it was three months before my 18th birthday and I heard stories about people dying and I didn't want to die before I turned 18, yet I still went to have it done. I was awake the entire time, because I didn't have enough money to pay for anesthesia, so I just kept hoping in my heart that things would go well and that I would be forgiven. Before I recovered from that abortion, my children's father and I were right back together again. It was like I wasted money and time because two months later, just after my 18th birthday, I was pregnant and going through the same thing. This time I spoke with him about getting an abortion, not because we were on bad terms or because I didn't want my child, but because of the sickness and stress levels that I experienced during my prior pregnancy. He agreed to come up with the money, so I scheduled an appointment to have it done. But, the week of that appointment I dreamt of having a little girl who was very healthy and beautiful, so I had a change of heart and made up my mind to have her. I went through my pregnancy well, other than being sick for the first four months. On May 5th, 1996, I gave birth to my third child, a baby girl. She was exactly as I saw in the dream, healthy and beautiful. From the time of her birth, my life was on a roller coaster ride—up and down, around and around, again and again, the same cycles repeated, breaking up with their father and experiencing intensive emotional struggles. Being 19 years old, a working mother of three, and a lover to their father with no directions or solid structure for my life was not an easy task. There were days of weakness that manifested through depression because I just did not know how to handle life's challenges. Alongside that depression came many days where my children witnessed my tears, anger and utter distress. Truth be told, there was time I took things out on them and felt so bad afterwards, but I really did not know how to address what needed fixing, so I never did.

  You would think that after all I had been through, I would have made sure to protect myself from getting pregnant again. Let me tell you that was not the case, instead I was pregnant again by age 21 and underwent another abortion, and again at 23, however that pregnancy I choose to have my baby. Carrying that child was totally different from all my other pregnancy experiences. I suffered with morning, noonday, and evening sickness literally every day. I was in and out of the hospital due to dehydration. After about the sixth time my doctor made me aware that my baby was taking every ounce of nutrients from my body so much that he was concerned about my well being, so he came up with a plan for me to receive home care until I could get through the stages of my sickness. So I was sent home with a PICC line intravenous (a long catheter that is inserted into a vein in your arm, leg, or neck); that PICC LINE was inserted into the right side of my neck. A nurse was assigned to visit me weekly to ensure the PICC line was professionally cleaned and flushed. There were days that my oldest child and my second oldest child had to bring me water or food out the kitchen, because I was too weak to move. Around about the fifth month, the sickness cleared up and thereafter my doctor released me from medical home care. I was never so happy to eat and move around. As I stated before, carrying him was totally different from any of my previous pregnancies. What I am about to say next is pure evidence that it was so. I had a bible that I never really used other than when I had migraine headaches and I'd placed it underneath my pillow; it felt comforting for me to sleep with. Well before I gave birth to him, a thought came to my mind to take my bible with me. On August 23, 2000, the day of his birth, I headed to the hospital for a scheduled Induction Labor. I was about 5 minutes away from home when I thought to turn around to get my bible from under my bed room pillow. I did not understand why until later on during my labor. Every time I had a sharp pain, I laid that bible open (to the book of Psalms Chapter 23) on my stomach. From that day to this one, I always felt in my heart that there was a purpose in doing that, so I call him my Psalm 23 son. After the birth of my fourth child, my life spiraled up and down, with attempts of trying to strive to be different so that my kids would not be neglected of things that I felt I did not get as a child. My heart was for my children to experience the true meaning of family. I had a made-up mind that I would never bring another man around my children, because I did not trust people with them. I was only twenty four, but my friends would always say that I acted like an old lady—which I did. I had a certain way I would move through life most of the time. I desired in my heart to embrace the wisdom of older women. I watched closely how they interacted with their children. I watched how they cooked and cleaned and how they purchased things in bulk to help save money; those and other learned experiences I applied to my life. Let me not forget to mention how I watched my Grandma push through severely tough times her entire life, so I incorporated things that I learned from her as well. However being twenty-four years old, living on my own with four kids (one in third grade, one in first grade, one in preschool and the other one in diapers,) while trying to be a wife to someone who had yet to make me his wife, and working sometimes two jobs, cleaning, doing laundry, and did I mention, that I also didn't quite know how to cook at the time, other than simple things? So, I'm pretty sure you can grasp my level of daily stress; did I say stress? Yes, I sure did.

    I was stressed for many reasons. For starters, I had underlying childhood issues that I was not aware of. The only thing I knew is that often my behavior signaled that something was wrong. The relationship with my partner appeared to function in a mostly dysfunctional way. We had more times apart than times together and even during our separations, those times were filled with unhealthy boundaries while we continued to behave as if we were still together.

The cycle of being in love one minute and being out of the love the next became a toxic and unhealthy pattern and I seemed to become addicted to living life that way. The mindset I adapted was an embittered one. Over the years of raising my children, I became bitter. This bitterness, however, was masked quite well because it only showed up within the walls of my home. This is why I called this chapter *A Bittersweet Journey*. My life as a mother who was bitter because of my past issues as a child; because of living in fornication; because of no education; because of my ongoing poor choices to live life my way rather than God's way. Somewhere, somehow, there were parts of me that never grew up mentally and emotionally and because of this I could only give my children the love language of physical love and financial support. There were many voids in my life, so my children were robbed of the areas they needed the most; however 20-plus years later I can truly admit that in spite of my choices and issues that made my life bitter, my four children were the sweetest part of my journey. They were always the reason why I never gave up on life—even when the voice of the enemy told me to. I vowed in my heart that I would never walk away and leave them to feel the pain I carried while growing up. I am humbly grateful that I was graced to never leave them, and I am more grateful that I lived to get a change to be healed (and continue to pray for the areas which may still need healing). I will forever be in a heart posture of thanksgiving for my bittersweet journey. It's one of the chapters in my life that made my story worth telling. I always say that when you take a road trip, you know exactly where you're going, but a journey is slightly different in that you may know where you'll start from, but you typically don't know where you will end up.

FINALLY FREE TO BE ME

    Upon conclusion of this chapter, I am excited to almost be at the finish line of revealing the fullness of the purpose of this book. So, I thank you in advance for preparing your heart as well. Let us keep going.... Two chapters left. From a bitter-sweet journey to--------------------turn the page to see....

4

AT THE END OF MY ROPE

April 29th, 2006 marked the beginning stages of coming to the end of my rope (a state in which one is not able to deal with their problems and difficult situations). I was thirty years old when I encountered one of the most challenging days of my life. It was just an hour or so before midnight when I received a phone call from my uncle's wife informing me that my grandfather, whom I called Daddy, was gone; he was dead. At first, as my partner and I rushed out the house to head over to my grandparents' home I thought to myself this must be a joke. While driving there, several thoughts ran through my mind; especially about the last time I saw him. A couple days prior to the day of that call, I was headed on a road trip to Orlando, Florida with some family members and before we left, we stopped by to see my grandparents. My grandfather gave me a very tight hug, upon him doing so I uttered these very words; "Daddy, you hugging me like I'm never coming back; I'm not moving away I'll be back", as I replayed those words in my mind I was disappointed with myself for not understanding the message in his tight hug was that he was moving away to his permanent home and that hug was the last hug I would ever receive from Him.

By the time we reached their home, all of my family had arrived. Once inside the house, I saw my grandfather laying on the living room sofa. In my mind I was still thinking this all has to be a big joke, he's sleeping like he normally does. So I walked over to him and called out his name "Daddy" but Daddy didn't answer, so I just sat on the floor next to him and put my head on his arm. In the meantime everything around me seemed to be moving in slow motion yet oddly at the same time fast-paced as I watched my grandmother, mother, uncles, my brothers try to come to grips with his passing and as I myself was thinking on how I would break the news to my children. I knew that they would take it extremely hard. On May 5, 2006, my daughter's birthday, my family put my grandfather (the only dad I knew) to rest. The death of my grandfather was like the rubber that met the road in my life. By August the grieving process of my grandfather's death brought on an added level of stress and depression as I battled thoughts of practically blaming myself for his death. Why would you battle that thought Tamika? You see, the day I went on that trip, I took that trip because I was going through my own life's foolishness and my grandparents knew the depths of what I was going through and they were concerned about me as well as my children. The battle in my mind was not expressed to anyone. I dared not share my pain with my family, who was processing their own pain and grief. I didn't have many people in my life that I would confide in, so I tried to deal with it on my own. I first tried overworking, shopping, and gambling. None of this worked. It only led me to sink deeper into the darkness I already struggled with. In other words, instead of me dealing with it; it was dealing with me as the voice of guilt and regret started talking very loudly accusing me of being a horrible granddaughter and saying that I should have been ashamed of the state my life was in when he passed and how he may have been disappointed with how my life turned out. I was angry with myself for never telling him or truly showing him that I appreciated him standing in the place of my father, for as much as he knew how to. This led me into a season of staying away from home everyday all day in order to try to cope with my emotions and to avoid having my children see that mom had lost what little control of her life she did have. Staying away from home seemed to work for only a short period of time thereafter I turned to porn as a way to cope. Nothing helped me, and before I knew it the passing of my grandfather caused me to become consumed with mental and emotional battles. One battle after another kept coming. I began comparing my partner to my grandfather—a man of few words, who always did what it took to ensure my grandmother was a happy woman. I expected my partner to become like my grandfather and when he failed to meet that expectation, I was very hurt. I'd get angry every time. My anger turned into rage and in my outbursts of rage l said every curse word that I could think of. I was uncontrollably disrespectful. Rage and anger had brought me to the point of existing, but not living. I would just go through the motions, emptiness was my portion, depletion became my first, middle, and last name. Mentally and emotionally, there was a huge blockage. The physical part of me now represented a walking dead person. The reality of my life was flashing before me in a way that it never did before. As I reflected upon having babies from the age of fifteen; being with their father for over 14 years, who had no plans at the time to marry me and even if he decided to, the man who stood as the father figure in my life was now gone and could not give me away in marriage; the memories of being a high school dropout saddened my heart; in addition, fear grabbed a hold of me as I looked in the faces of my children who were growing older and how I was hurting them. I also felt terrible about living in fornication. I was over thirty and had no driver's license. I was only able to get jobs making eight dollars an hour. I never thought about the future of my kids; I didn't know the importance of making sure they were able to face this world with healthy mindsets. I didn't understand that my mental and emotional battles were a battle for them, too. While I was caught up in my selfishness, my children suffered the reality of so many of the things that were troubling me. When I think back to that time, I truly believe that the grieving process of my grandfather almost led me to a nervous breakdown. The mental and emotional battle started in 2006 and went on for three years. Those three years seemed as if it was triple the time. I personally don't wish that anyone would have to go through that experience. I know personally the feelings of being alive yet feeling dead; having every reason around to be hopeful, yet feeling hopeless. It's not a good feeling at all. Having been in that state for three years as I entered the year of 2009, somehow I developed a feeling that I was missing something. I started speaking out loud that I am a good person, but I was missing church. I spoke it on a regular basis. At that time, I was totally unaware that we have what we say. All I knew was that my life seemed to be a big mess, but I didn't know how to change it. Please permit me to be transparent to say that I should have been treated for clinical mental illness simply because depression didn't just show up at age 30, it showed up very early in my childhood and because I was unable to identify it as depression, it had its way in my life. I now have reasons to believe that it may have been a generational trait; even now, looking at the film projector of my life, I have to say that the three series of chapters in my life: defenseless childhood attack; the seeds of the enemy; and the bittersweet journey all played a major part in coming to the end of my rope and brought me to a place of being tired of everything. I was sick and tired of being sick and tired. I couldn't hold on to the way my life was any longer. I was a person who masked myself very well, but let me tell you the masks were coming off even when I didn't take them off—as I became more and more tired of the state I was in. Everywhere I went, my pain and depression showed up. As I looked upon the lives of others who seemed to be functioning healthily, becoming full of jealousy, I then worked hard to paint myself as this picture perfect woman, mother, and lover. Doing so only made the conditions of my mental and emotional state worse. I became numb to life itself... I desperately needed help. Coming to the end of my rope was a state in my life where I could not take any more of life's pain—it was live or die. I didn't want to die, but I didn't know how to live... have you ever been in this place before or do you know someone that has? If so, then you can relate to what I'm saying and if not chances are you can't. Either way I would love for you to press through to the last chapter to see how my story will end from the end of my rope to _____ .....

5

RESCUED FROM THE HANDS OF MY ENEMY

One of the most touching examples of being rescued is that of one who has been intentionally locked up in a burning house by an enemy who wanted them dead; without anyone else being aware that they were locked up in the fire and about to die, and their only hope of survival was that someone on the outside heard them crying out for HELP and either comes to rescue them or calls 911, and as a result of HELP arriving they come out of the burning house alive.

Listen, I've never been in an actual burning fire, so to fathom the pain that someone feels who is stuck in a fire isn't easy to think about without tearing up. Even more challenging is trying to comprehend the thoughts of that person. I'm sure the level of trauma to the brain caused by the tormenting fear of not making it out alive, the unbearable amount of pain the body may experience, the assumptions that every second may seem like an hour, every minute may seem like a month and even the thought of being speechless at the time of their rescue, but somewhere in their mind and heart there are words of thanksgiving.

Although I haven't physically experienced it, I can relate to that example simply because spiritually my entire life felt like I lived amidst a burning fire set by the enemy (Satan). As far back as I can recall, my struggles felt like I was in a blaze of fire and about to die.

The latter of 2009 was the year of rescue for me. It started just a month after my thirty-third birthday. I was on a football field in a local community where my children played football when I meet this Lady named "Annette Woods"—now Annette Mitchell. She was a parent of one of the kids that I had submitted to being a team mom for. She and I connected from time-to-time, by phone. At the end of the football season, we teamed up to accomplish our team goals for the end of the year celebration that was done on a yearly quarter. One day, she asked me to visit her church. I didn't visit her church until January 31, 2010, but when I did it was right on time. The name of that church is called Bread of Life Christian Center founded by Pastor George and First Lady Jestina Bowles.

The message that was being taught by Pastor Bowles was that of the woman at the well. At the end of church service, he conducted an altar call which drew me to the altar to receive salvation. This was the fourth or fifth time in my life that I openly confessed the Lord Jesus Christ as my Savior, but despite doing so prior times, there was absolutely no change. It was as if nothing took place. I am so glad to confess that this time was different. Pastor Bowles' message represented the name of His church so powerfully "Bread of Life" it was the bread of life for sure (God's word) and it tasted so good. I had never tasted anything quite like it.

I didn't understand it. All I knew was that I wanted more of that taste. So from that day on, a turning point happened in my life. I began attending church every time the church doors opened, and this time I stayed with God. It might have been due to the soul cry inside of me. I was crying out saying somebody please help me and I had stumbled across the very help that I needed. How do I know this? Well, let's just say that I started noticing things were happening to me I didn't understand, but I knew it wasn't man's doing. Some examples are that I was remembering songs from when I hung out with my friends whose parents were pastors and scriptures like Psalm 23 and Psalm 27 and Psalm 91 that were given after my first pregnancy at age 13. I recalled the respect and honor given to God when people came into His house back then they would kneel as a sign of reverence unto God when they entered a church. I was also reminded of sins that I needed to repent of and ask for forgiveness of—the anger and rage that came out of me at times with my children; the stealing that I did; the abortions I had; the lies I told; the foul language (cursing) I used—the spirit of repentance was heavily upon me. God was speaking to me so loud and clear in ways that only I could comprehend (He meets everyone where they are because of this it didn't take long for my zeal for GOD to turn on and stay on). I was much like the woman at the well whom Jesus told her everything about herself, and she went out to share it with an entire town of people. That was me. I was attentive and quick to obey pretty much everything my pastor taught. There were times just before he taught his message that he would say he's the shoe salesman and we were the customers. He also said that we had to be reasonable for putting on the right size shoe (meaning take the word and cause it to fit into your life for that time and season). I walked in several pairs of shoes. Some of them were the right size, while others were too big. Nevertheless, inside my heart I was convinced each time that I was wearing the right shoe size, but what I didn't know was that the same enemy that attacked me from birth and held me captive to age thirty three wasn't going stop his attempts just because I was now saved and that he would work even harder. I learned this during the many trials and tribulations that I went through. I assumed that life after salvation would not have any mental or emotional problems, no pain or issues. I had no knowledge at all that once I received salvation; I needed to go through the process of deliverance. I was in pretty bad shape prior to being rescued; living a life in total captivity and total bondage. I needed a lot of deliverance, especially with strongholds. Strongholds of the mind are established thoughts that we count as true, but actually are a false belief. It is lies that come from the father of lies (Satan) and once we receive and believe the lies, they affect our emotions and behaviors. The revelation of strongholds being in my life came to me by the way of being a part of a church service that was teaching on salvation. The message of salvation convicted me about the lifestyle of fornication, also known as a soul tie. Both are used when describing a spiritual connection between two people. Most times, it is said to come into existence after two people have been physically intimate before marriage. In others, it is said to form after an intensely close spiritual or emotional relationship.

What do you know? That message hit me to my core and got me to thinking about the 20 years I lived in fornication, so I gave that up. In doing so, my lifelong partner and I got married on March 26, 2011. However, there was a lot of baggage that came from the soul tie that I hadn't got healed from that showed up in our marriage. The pain of our past relationship was speaking louder than any possible success for our future, the battle to press beyond our pain seemed impossible to bear. I became weaker in my flesh nature and eventually in September 2011 we separated. I then went into a stage of depression that lasted for months it was so heavy in my life, however I masked it well and when I couldn't mask it I hid from others. The thought to stop going to church increased during those times, but a voice deep inside of me was saying don't stop so I kept attending. Although I kept going, that didn't stop the enemy of my past. He kept attacking my mind and emotions with concerns of my partner being gone, my father not wanting me, my children not having the life that God required me to give them; because of these thoughts, my emotions went on a roller coaster ride. The impact of all this tempted me to think that I was crazy. I received those thoughts and began to believe them, and that left me questioning my salvation. I had thoughts like you belong to Satan still and you're a hopeless case. This lasted until one night I was crying in my bed fighting back those thoughts when I was feeling pressured by my flesh to utter the words that I am crazy. I laid in bed with the pillow over my head almost about to say those words when another thought came to me to pick up the phone and admit myself in a mental place but hallelujah, thank you Jesus! Just then, a third thought came to me to get in my closet, so I did. I was in a fetal position in my closet I laid there for about ten minutes then it came to me to scream out loud and say that I am not crazy. So I did just that until I felt those nagging thoughts leave me. Then I went to bed. I now understand that it was God himself releasing his deliverance and healing in my life. <u>He</u> even gave me a promise that <u>He</u> began a good work in me and <u>He</u> will complete it.

    Not long after, while I was at the beach sitting on a rock, trying to clear my head, I heard the voice of God say *"confess your faults one to another"*. Inwardly I asked, how can I do that when no one was there with me? He answered by saying, "The Father, Son, and Holy Spirit is here". Suddenly, the words "I hate him" came to my heart to confess, but instead I blurted "I can't say that to God, He wont approve!" However I confessed to God that I felt I hated my husband and tears began to flood my face; then the voice of God said to me "The earth is the Lord's and the fullness thereof and he who dwells in it". He then said to me "the King of Glory shall come in". He said, "daughter, you need to learn how to live." The work of deliverance was taking place in my life. Not long after that He opened the portal for another phase of healing as I stopped at a local gas station. Upon entering, I met face-to-face with the man who I previously mentioned violated me as a child while I slept. As much as I wanted to tell him a *thang* or two, when he asked me how I was doing, all God allowed me to say was, "I'm saved Now and I'm doing well." Thereafter came another phase of healing that I was not expecting. One day at church, my pastor was praying, while praying the Holy Spirit permitted him to say these words he said "some of you need to come to the altar and release whoever you have not forgiven" as he was speaking by the power of the Holy Spirit, I was processing his words in my mind. In my heart, I began speaking to God and said "I don't think that I have unforgiveness because I admitted to you that I had developed hatred in my heart towards my husband, because of the things he and I had been through, and I just saw that guy who attempted to violate me sexually and I didn't feel hate in my heart", but at that moment God prompted my pastor to say "you may need to ask God to show you who" so immediately, I ran to the altar, fell to my knees, and asked God "who is it?" Shockingly, I clearly heard the words it is your father. I never once thought I held unforgiveness towards him. I thought because I did not know him I felt nothing; well, the one who knows the heart of every man knew differently. He revealed to me how I held unforgiveness in my heart towards my father; He knew I blamed him for all the violating things that happened to me and that I was angry at him for robbing me of the joy a little girl's heart longs to feel when she hears her daddy's voice saying she his little princess, this one act of obedience resulted into my father contacting me 3 days later. He asked to speak with me so that he could get some things right with me before he left this earth. I agreed to speak with him and from that day onwards; I have been on a road of healing; I have forgiven him, and there's nothing ungodly in my heart towards him. As a matter of fact, I never thought I would call him dad but God has changed my mind and heart. Not only that, but on June 10th 2019, I was at work when I took a restroom break I checked my phone and to my surprise I received a text message from my father that said Happy Birthday Daughter you'll always be daddy's princess I love you! Those words were worth more than every material gift that I received that year. When I sat down at my desk, God whispered to me, "Tamika Baldwin, I love you so much that I gave my son for you. Nothing happened in your life that I did not know about. At age thirty-three I called you out of darkness into my marvelous light and since then I have been drawing you with my love and kindness," He said "my daughter, I will never leave you nor forsake you, I have plans to prosper you and to give you an expected end" as GOD was speaking to me I was writing as fast as I could and I recall fighting back my tears because I didn't want my coworkers to see me crying so I got up and went back to the restroom to gather myself. I lifted my hands and said "thank you Jesus." Upon returning to my seat. God still wasn't finished speaking to me. He then gave me the revelation that He knew I loved Him and had been working hard to prove my love for Him, but He wanted me to receive His love for me... He informed that a father's love is the first love that a young girl experiences and if it is given in a healthy way it is easier for her to receive the love of God. He informed me that mental and emotional healing and breakthroughs were being released into my life. Thereafter I heard these words: "Finally Free to Be Me". Later on that day, God gave me 5 statements. I wasn't certain of why until, about three months later, my father sent me a text message about a publishing company that he found and he thought I should check it out. At that very moment, I was reminded of how much I had been journaling since my salvation transition and how, in those times, I had several thoughts and dreams to write a book.

After work, I rushed home and gathered all my notes. As I reviewed them, I felt I should, but I didn't believe that I could so I just pondered it in my heart. In the meantime, I was chasing hard after God and writing a lot of prayers. I became more serious about serving God in church, dancing for the Lord and just committing to anything I felt compelled of the Lord to do. While doing so, I still struggled many days, but I knew God had spoken to my heart and no matter how much the enemy came to tell me differently, I held on to that which I knew GOD said. Even during the most challenging times, like the enemy attacking my children, the ones who I love more than anyone outside of GOD. Other times I struggled in the areas of poverty and lack, going without people and things that I thought I could not live without. However, a light switch flicked in my heart one day in April of 2020, and I stayed up all night praising God until I fell asleep. Upon waking the next morning, God downloaded a message that would change my life forever, He said to me, "by the reason of your afflictions you cried out to me, I heard your cry." He then said "my daughter you have suffered for a while now I am about to settle you." He said, "Tamika Baldwin's history was full of mental and emotional bondage that came as a result of generational bloodline sins & personal willful sinning." He then said "even while you were a sinner I was there with you. The times you thought you would lose your mind—I kept your mind. The times when your emotions told you life wasn't worth living, or that nobody loved you—I was right there. I would not allow you to give up or give in because I already had a plan for you to win." He said "daughter I'm about to change your history, one thing I need for you to do is hold on to the horns of salvation", then He gave me a song of comfort called *Cried My Last Tear* by Bishop Paul Morton. I googled that song and I released tears of hope as I heard the verse that said *"I don't know what he's going to do, but I know it's going to work out for you so go on and cry; let it all out; cry your last tear it's going to be alright"* and in my heart, at that very moment I believed that GOD was going to completely heal me of all the pain of my past—the guilt and shame, the rejection, neglect, depression, low self-esteem, insecurities, fears, and unworthiness. I also believed that because of the blood shed of Jesus on the cross of Calvary that I would fully overcome. My heart became so full of the joy, strength, and hope of God that I began reflecting on all that He had already brought me through and His promises that say He would work all things together for the good of them that love Him and that are called according to his purpose. I was reminded of his promise, which says he would restore my youth. As I thought on these promises, I couldn't help but think of how he helped me go back to school after 20+ years and receive my high school diploma; how he allowed me to live and get some things right with my kids (I'm still doing so by His grace); and to do better with my grandchildren. I was so in tuned with reflecting on His love and faithfulness and how He kept me throughout my struggles in life. The more He ministered to my heart as I was reflecting on these things, I began writing them and used a journal my nephew had blessed me with for mother's day; I jotted down everything that I believe God was speaking into my life. On May 20, 2020, He spoke to me and told me to write down 7+7+7 as I did I said to him, "GOD that equals 21 what are you saying to me?", he then replied, " go look at your calendar and count 21 days from today", so I did and to my surprise the 21st day landed on my birthday. I smile and said, "God you have a sense of humor for sure" (I used to think my birthday was a curse to me because of the hand life had dealt me—boy did God teach me differently!) He then said to me, "Tamika now that you're ready to receive I'm about to show you just how wide my love is for you..." **CAN I TELL YOU THAT GOD IS ONE WITH HIS WORD**! He doesn't lie nor does He change his mind. I can say this because He did just that, from that day until the day of my birthday He unfolded the depth of his love towards me through words of encouragement, prayers, messages of faith, songs of deliverance, and confirmations of healing in my life. One day, just days before my birthday, as I walked through the neighborhood I grew up in talking to God he instructed me to walk to the apartment complex I lived in when my life transitioned from being a troubled youth into a bittersweet journey. That complex has two entrances: a front and a back. I planned to walk out the back entrance, but I felt God wanted me to walk out the entrance that I came in which was the front entrance. The very moment that I walked out it poured down rain. I heard God say to me "DAUGHTER, I am washing away your past." I cried and then called my nephew, who had gifted me the journal for Mother's Day. I explained to him how that journal was an avenue of release as I wrote down all my brokenness and everything that GOD was speaking to me. I thanked him for his obedience in gifting it to me. That same day, I received a phone call from a dear friend of mine, whose house I would clean around the same time every year, (that time was normally during the summer) this year she offered me to stay as a guest in her home and use her car the entire month. This worked out good for me, because I had planned to go check in at a hotel to have some me and Jesus time, instead I stayed at her home. I found out that God arranged for me to be there as my birthday fell on a Wednesday, so I made plans to celebrate the weekend of that day which was June 12th-June 14th.

Saturday June 12th, I got up prayed and started my day just enjoying the blessing of seeing another year. I had a photo shoot scheduled, something I had planned to do way back in 2013 when I received my High School Diploma, but I didn't do it—howbeit, delay is never denial. I really enjoyed that moment. The photographer played worship songs the entire time, and I worshiped the Lord while taking my pictures. I then went out to eat and headed back to my friends' house. Upon my arrival I thought to check her mailbox and bring her mail inside—this was something that I never did before. I got the mail and put it on her kitchen counter. I then prepared myself to get ready for bed. Before doing so, I returned to the kitchen for a drink and noticed that a paper had fallen on the floor. I picked it up and placed it back on the counter, went to lie down only to feel the need to get back up again, the paper was on the floor and this time it came to me to open the paper and read it and when I did all I could do was look shocked. It was a letter then the thought came to me look at the top of the paper read it slowly when I saw the date and written message on the paper I knew that God prepared it for me; the date was June 10th and the message said Jesus loves you, immediately God reminded me of His promise to show me how deep his love was for me...

This letter had me in tears there were two scriptures written on that paper the one that spoke to me was Matthew 9:1-2. This is when I really knew I'm to tell my story all for God's glory; *Finally Free To Be Me*. I am no longer the defenseless child; the seed of the enemy can no longer grow in my life; the bittersweet journey converted pain for gain, being at the end of my rope had purpose and destiny attached to it;

FINALLY FREE TO BE ME

Finally Free to Be Me is God's divine victory for me (a verse of song call Worth - from Anthony Brown & group therapy)— *He thought I was worth saving, so he came and changed my life; He thought I was keeping, so He cleaned me up inside; He thought I was to die for; so he sacrificed His life so I can be free; so I can be whole and so I can tell everyone I know.* Hallelujah; Glory to the God who changed my life. I bow to give him the glory. He is the reason I can write freely and I'm looking forward to being all that He's called me to be. I pray my story will help someone to know that Jesus truly came to set the captives free.

PRAYER
LORD, SET ME FREE TO BE ME

Heavenly Father, there is so much about my life and the purpose for my existence that I do not yet understand. So right now I am trusting that you will hear my petition and open my eyes to see and to fully embrace your vision for my life. I often feel like I am battling things I don't even comprehend, while each day I strive for a better tomorrow. Some days are heavier than I care to admit. Some days I feel at the end of my rope. Some days I question everything. So, I now humble myself to your divine guidance. Wherever in my life I have made a mess, I have allowed sin to reign, or I have given place to addictions and bad habits, please help me to make better quality decisions. I repent for allowing those things into my life and for living contrary to your will. I'm sorry for not considering you when I make decisions or am impulsive. I truly desire to make the kind of choices that will please you and align with your purpose for my life. I believe in your word that says, "So if the Son sets you free, you will be free indeed." I desire the liberty and freedom to be free to walk as the person who "you" divinely created me to be, and not the person who society deemed I should be. I now understand that becoming that person will require dedication and devotion on my part and I am willing. I simply ask that you show me how to Finally Be Free to be Me–the Me you intended. I remain open to recieve your answers in my life however you decide to impart them. I promise to do my best to identify your leading and to obey and follow through.
In the Precious Name of Jesus, Amen.

ABOUT THE AUTHOR

Tamika Baldwin is a born-again believer. Her rebirth encounter took place January 31, 2010 under the Leadership of Pastor George and First Lady Jestina Bowles at Bread of Life Christian Center. After starting her journey of New life in Christ, she went back to school in 2013 and successfully earned her High School Diploma at Atlantic Technical Trade School. She completed and received a Home Health Aide Certificate December of 2019 at Palm Beach County, Boca Helping Hands. She is currently using her learned skills as a Home Health Aide to serve and care for her eighty-five-year old grandmother. She Graduated in 2020 from Daughter's of Zion Mentorship Program and was elected most congenial mentee.

Her favorite scripture is 1st Peter 2:9 But ye are a chosen generation, a royal priesthood, an holy nation, a peculiar people; that ye should show forth the praises of him who hath called you out of darkness into his marvelous light.

She is an honorable loving mother of four children as well as a proud grandmother of seven grandchildren. She currently resides in South Florida and has gracefully and faithfully stayed the course of submitting to Leadership at Bread of Life Christian Center for the past eleven years, where she has devoted her time to serve as a Pulpit Assistant, on the Prayer Team, Hospitality Team, Ministry in Dance, as well as to the Youth Ministry.

www.ingramcontent.com/pod-product-compliance
Lightning Source LLC
Chambersburg PA
CBHW052123110526
44592CB00013B/1729